Science

GRADE 1

Steck-Vaughn
School Supply

CORE SKILLS

Contents

www.harcourtschoolsupply.com
© Houghton Mifflin Harcourt Publishing Company

Table of Contents
Core Skills Science, G1 SV 9781419098413

Introduction

Steck-Vaughn's *Core Skills Science* series offers parents and educators high-quality, curriculum-based products that align with the Common Core Standards for Reading in the Sciences for grades 1–6. The *Core Skills Science* books provide informative and grade-appropriate readings on a wide variety of topics in life, earth, and physical science. Two pages of worksheets follow each reading passage. The book includes:

- clear illustrations, making scientific concepts accessible to young learners

- engaging reading passages, covering a wide variety of topics in life, earth, and physical science

- logically sequenced activities, transitioning smoothly from basic comprehension to higher-order thinking skills

- reading skills, ascertaining that children understand what they have read

- vocabulary activities, challenging children to show their understanding of scientific terms

- critical thinking activities, increasing children's ability to analyze, synthesize, and evaluate scientific information

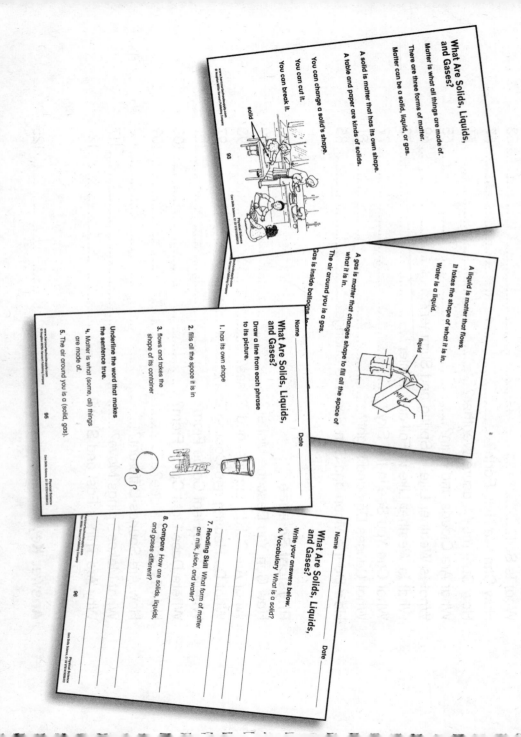

What Are the Parts of Plants?

Plants have parts.

Each part helps in a different way.

Roots take in water.

Roots hold the plant in the ground.

A stem joins parts of plants.

Stems carry water from the roots to other parts.

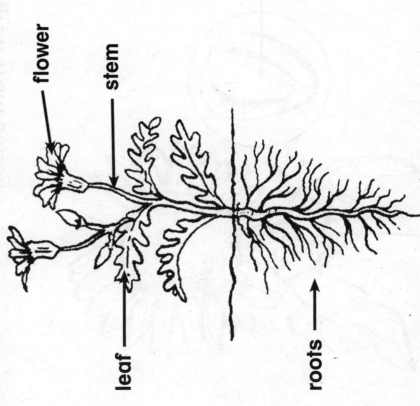

flower

stem

leaf

roots

www.harcourtschoolsupply.com
© Houghton Mifflin Harcourt Publishing Company

Life Science
Core Skills Science, G1 SV 9781419098413

Most plants have leaves.

Leaves make food for the plant.

Leaves also make oxygen.

People and animals need oxygen.

Many plants have flowers.

A flower makes seeds.

New plants grow from seeds.

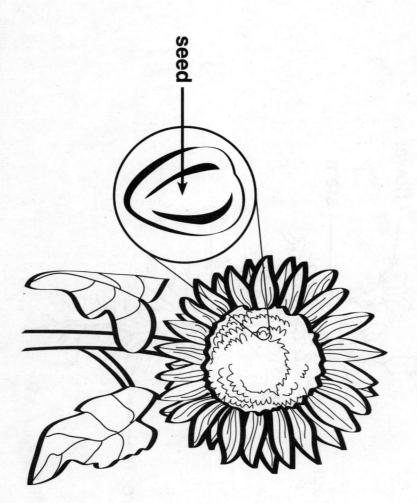

seed

Name _____

Date _____

What Are the Parts of Plants?

Draw a line from each definition to a part of the plant.

1. Takes in water from the ground

2. Connects roots to other plant parts

3. Makes food

4. Makes seeds

Underline the word that makes the sentence true.

5. (Stems, Leaves) carry water from the roots to other plant parts.

6. (Flowers, Leaves) give off oxygen that people and animals breathe.

www.harcourtschoolsupply.com
© Houghton Mifflin Harcourt Publishing Company

7

Life Science
Core Skills Science, G1 SV 9781419098413

What Are the Parts of Plants?

Write your answers below.

7. Vocabulary What are roots?

_____

_____

_____

8. Reading Skill Why are a plant's
roots under the ground?

_____

_____

_____

9. Observe Which plant parts can you
observe above the ground?

_____

_____

_____

How Can Plants Be Sorted?

You can sort plants.

You can put plants in groups by their parts.

Some plants have sharp points called spines.

A cactus has spines.

Some plants have flat leaves.

Many indoor plants have flat leaves.

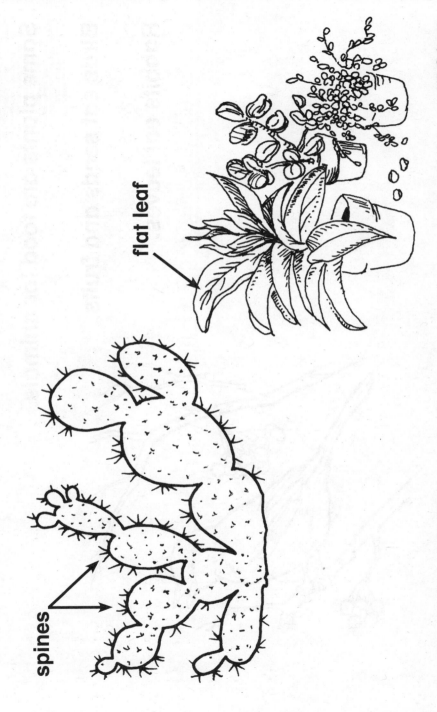

spines

flat leaf

Life Science

Core Skills Science, G1 SV 9781419098413

www.harcourtschoolsupply.com

© Houghton Mifflin Harcourt Publishing Company

Some plants are food for people.

People eat leaves.

Lettuce is a leaf.

People eat fruit.

An apple is a fruit.

Some plants are food for animals.

Birds eat seeds and fruits.

Rabbits eat leaves.

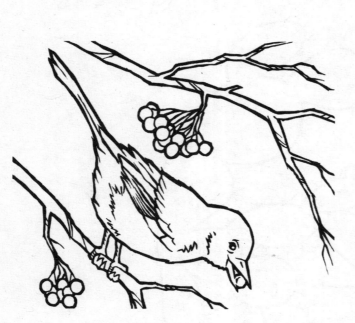

www.harcourtschoolsupply.com
© Houghton Mifflin Harcourt Publishing Company

Name _____

Date _____

How Can Plants Be Sorted?

Draw a line from each sentence to its picture.

1. This plant has spines.

2. This plant has flat leaves.

Underline the word that makes the sentence true.

3. You can sort plants by looking at their (colors, parts).

4. Some plants are food for (other plants, people).

5. Some animals eat (seeds, spines) for food.

www.harcourtschoolsupply.com
© Houghton Mifflin Harcourt Publishing Company

Life Science
Core Skills Science, G1 SV 9781419098413

How Can Plants Be Sorted?

Write your answers below.

6. Vocabulary What kind of plant has spines?

_____

7. Reading Skill What are three plant parts
that animals eat?

_____

_____

8. Compare How are plants different?

_____

_____

_____

How Do Plants Change As They Grow?

Pine trees start as seeds.

Pine seeds are in a cone.

A seed grows into a seedling.

The seedling grows into a tree.

The tree grows cones.

Seeds are in the cones.

Pine trees start as seeds.

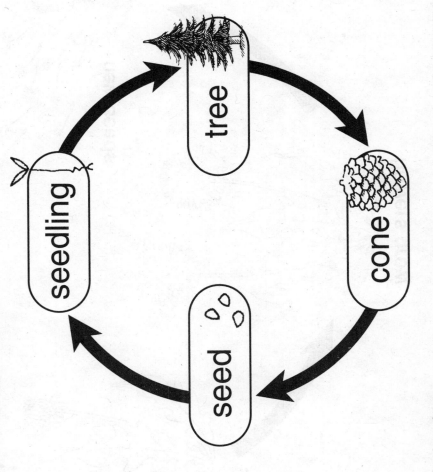

www.harcourtschoolsupply.com
© Houghton Mifflin Harcourt Publishing Company

Life Science
Core Skills Science, G1 SV 9781419098413

Changes in plants and animals happen in an order called a life cycle.

Different plants have different life cycles.

Look at the model.

The model shows the life cycle of a plant.

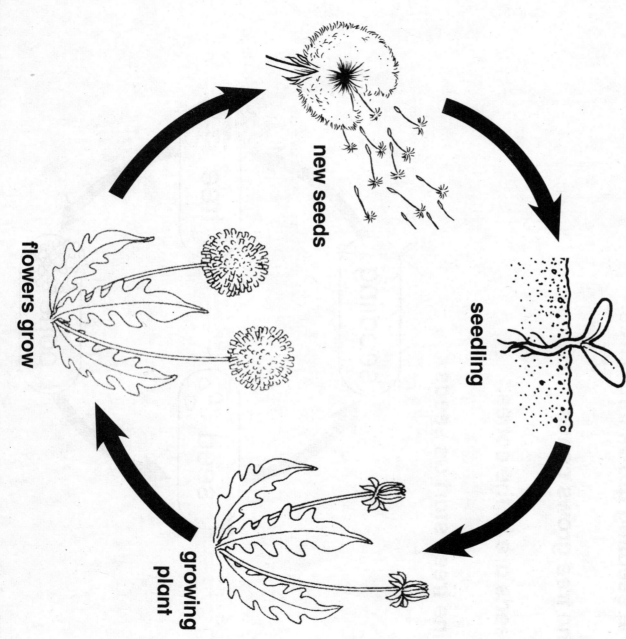

new seeds

seedling

growing plant

flowers grow

Name

Date

How Do Plants Change As They Grow?

1. Draw a box around the picture of a cone.

2. Circle the picture of a seedling.

3. Draw a triangle around some seeds.

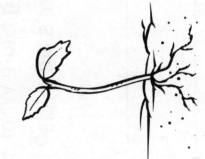

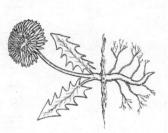

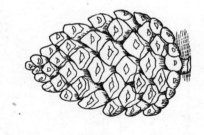

www.harcourtschoolsupply.com
© Houghton Mifflin Harcourt Publishing Company

Life Science
Core Skills Science, G1 SV 9781419098413

How Do Plants Change As They Grow?

Write your answers below.

4. Vocabulary What is a cone?

_____

_____

5. Reading Skill What comes after the seed in a plant's life cycle?

_____

_____

6. Use Models How can a model help you learn about a plant's life cycle?

_____

_____

_____

www.harcourtschoolsupply.com
© Houghton Mifflin Harcourt Publishing Company

Life Science
Core Skills Science, G1 SV 9781419098413

How Do Animals Use Their Parts?

Animals have body parts.

**Some body parts help
animals find food.**

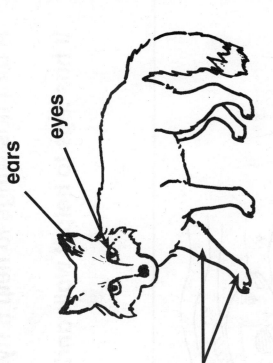

ears

eyes

legs and paws

**Some body parts help
animals stay safe.**

stinger

**Some body parts help
animals hide.**

fur color

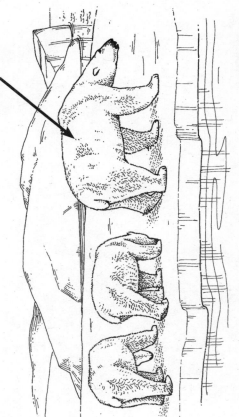

www.harcourtschoolsupply.com
© Houghton Mifflin Harcourt Publishing Company

Some body parts help animals move.

A bird has wings to help it fly.

It has legs to help it walk and hop.

A fish has a tail and fins to help it swim.

A lion has legs to help it run fast.

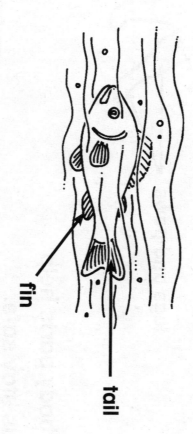

fin

tail

Name _____ Date _____

How Do Animals Use Their Parts?

_____ | _____

1. Write the word *wings* under the animal that has wings.

2. Write the word *fins* under the animal that has fins.

3. Write the word *legs* under the animals that have legs.

4. Write the word *swim* under the animal that lives in water.

5. Write the word *run* under the animal that can run.

Life Science

Core Skills Science, G1 SV 9781419098413

www.harcourtschoolsupply.com

© Houghton Mifflin Harcourt Publishing Company

Name _____ Date _____

How Do Animals Use Their Parts?

Write your answers below.

6. Vocabulary How do fins help a fish?

_____

_____

7. Reading Skill What body parts help an animal find food?

_____

_____

8. Infer How does a stinger help an animal stay safe?

_____

_____

Core Skills Science, G1 SV 9781419098413

Life Science

How Are Animals Grouped?

Scientists put animals into groups.

One group is called mammals.

Most mammals have hair or fur.

All mammals have lungs to help them breathe.

A baby mammal drinks milk from its mother.

A lion is a mammal.

You are a mammal, too.

Another group is birds.

Birds have wings and feathers.

Birds have lungs to help them breathe.

www.harcourtschoolsupply.com
© Houghton Mifflin Harcourt Publishing Company

Another group is fish.

Fish live in water.

Fish have gills to help them breathe.

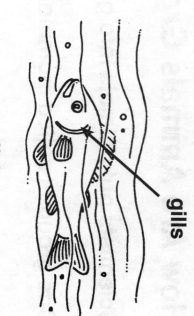

fish

gills

Another group is reptiles.

A reptile has dry skin with scales.

Lizards and snakes are reptiles.

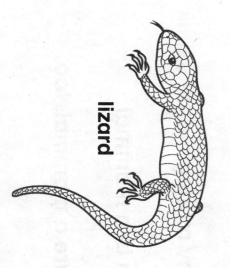

lizard

Another group is amphibians.

An amphibian has wet skin.

Frogs and toads are amphibians.

frog

Name _____

Date _____

How Are Animals Grouped?

1. Label each picture with a word from the box.

| mammal   fish   amphibian   bird   reptile |

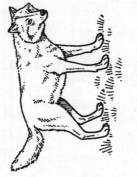

_____

_____

_____

_____

_____

2. Circle the animal above that has feathers.

3. Draw a triangle around the animal above that has gills.

Life Science

Core Skills Science, G1 SV 9781419098413

www.harcourtschoolsupply.com
© Houghton Mifflin Harcourt Publishing Company

Name _____ Date _____

How Are Animals Grouped?

Write your answers below.

4. Vocabulary What are gills?

_____

_____

5. Reading Skill How are birds and mammals alike?

_____

_____

6. Infer Which animal is an amphibian— a snake, a frog, or a fish?

_____

_____

What Can People Do?

People have many body parts.

Body parts help you do things.

You use your arms to hug.

You use your legs to walk.

Some body parts help you learn what is around you.

These body parts are your senses.

You have five senses.

Ears let
you hear.

A nose lets
you smell.

A mouth lets
you taste.

Eyes let
you see.

Hands let
you feel.

www.harcourtschoolsupply.com
© Houghton Mifflin Harcourt Publishing Company

Life Science
Core Skills Science, G1 SV 9781419098413

People grow and change.

First you were a baby.

Then you grew to be a child.

Someday you will become an adult.

You must stay healthy to keep growing.

You need to eat good food.

You need to exercise to be strong.

You need to sleep to rest your body and mind.

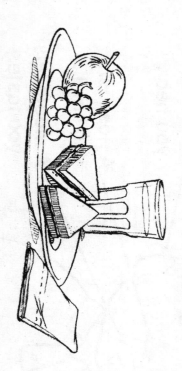

What Can People Do?

Draw a line to show the body part being used.

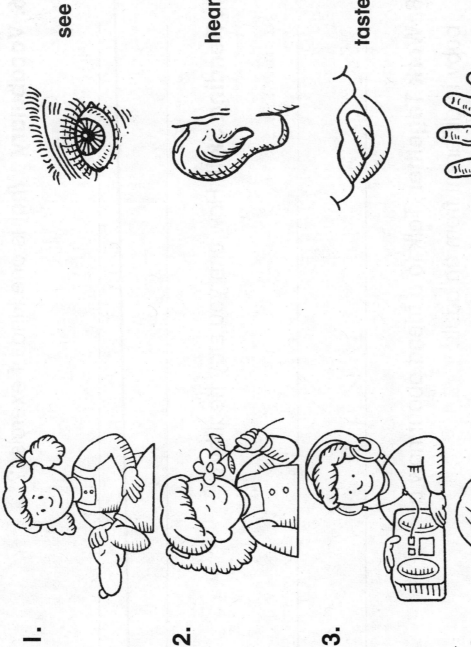

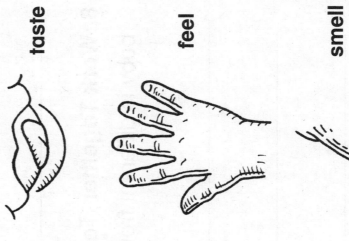

see

hear

taste

feel

smell

1.

2.

3.

4.

5.

www.harcourtschoolsupply.com
© Houghton Mifflin Harcourt Publishing Company

Life Science
Core Skills Science, G1 SV 9781419098413

What Can People Do?

Write your answers below.

6. Vocabulary What is one kind of exercise?

_____

_____

7. Reading Skill How can you stay healthy?

_____

_____

8. Work Together Talk to a friend about how a baby is different from an adult.

_____

_____

_____

What Is a Living Thing?

A living thing grows and changes.

It makes other living things that are like it.

It needs air and food.

It needs water and space.

People and animals are living things.

Trees and grass are living things, too.

www.harcourtschoolsupply.com
© Houghton Mifflin Harcourt Publishing Company

Core Skills Science, G1 SV 9781419098413
Life Science

Some things are not alive.

They are nonliving things.

A nonliving thing does not eat or drink.

It does not grow.

It does not make other living things that are like it.

It does not need air, food, and water.

nonliving thing

living thing

Name _____ Date _____

What Is a Living Thing?

Draw a line from each sentence to its picture.

1. Living things grow and change.

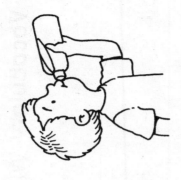

2. Living things need food.

3. Living things need water.

4. Living things make other living things.

Life Science SV 9781419098413
Core Skills Science, G1

What Is a Living Thing?

Write your answers below.

5. Vocabulary What is a living thing?

_____

_____

6. Reading Skill Name three nonliving things.

_____

_____

7. Classify Is water a living thing or a nonliving thing? Explain your answer.

_____

_____

_____

www.harcourtschoolsupply.com
© Houghton Mifflin Harcourt Publishing Company

What Do Living Things Need?

Plants and animals need food.

Plants use sunlight, air, and water to make their own food.

Some animals eat plants.

Some animals eat other animals.

Many animals eat both plants and animals.

Plants and animals need water.

Most plants get water from the ground.

Many animals get water by drinking.

Plants and animals need air.

Animals breathe air.

Plants use air to make food.

Plants and animals need space.

Plants need space to grow.

Animals need space to find food.

Animals need shelter.

Shelter is a safe place to live.

Name _____

Date _____

What Do Living Things Need?

1. Circle the picture that shows what plants need to make food.

2. Draw a plus sign (+) on the picture that shows an animal getting food.

3. Draw a line through the picture that shows an animal finding shelter.

4. Draw a box around the picture that shows an animal getting water.

www.harcourtschoolsupply.com
© Houghton Mifflin Harcourt Publishing Company

35

Life Science

Core Skills Science, G1 SV 9781419098413

www.harcourtschoolsupply.com
© Houghton Mifflin Harcourt Publishing Company

Name _____   Date _____

What Do Living Things Need?

Write your answers below.

5. Vocabulary What kinds of food do

animals eat?

_____

_____

6. Reading Skill What do plants need to live?

_____

_____

7. Observe Look at the picture.
What need is the child taking
care of?

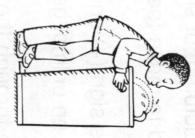

_____

_____

What Lives in Forests?

A forest is a place with many trees.

The trees grow close together.

Animals use the living things in a forest.

Animals use the nonliving things, too.

They use these things for food and shelter.

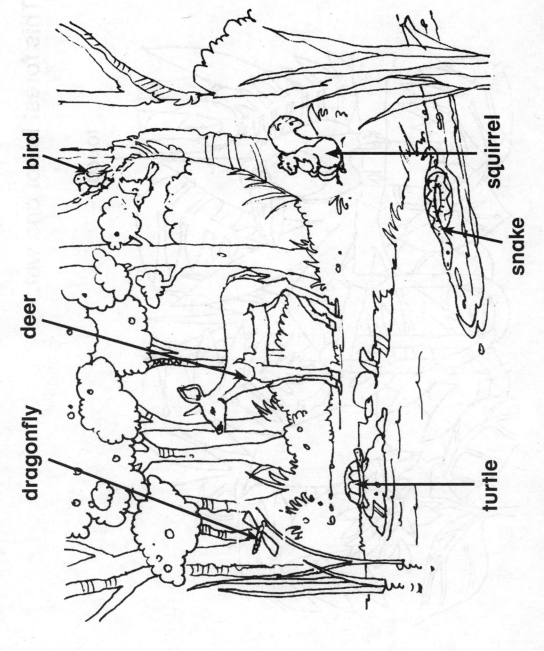

dragonfly

deer

bird

squirrel

snake

turtle

Life Science
Core Skills Science, G1 SV 9781419098413

There are many kinds of forests.

Some are hot and wet.

Some are cold and dry.

Different plants live in each forest.

Different animals live in each forest.

This forest is hot and wet.

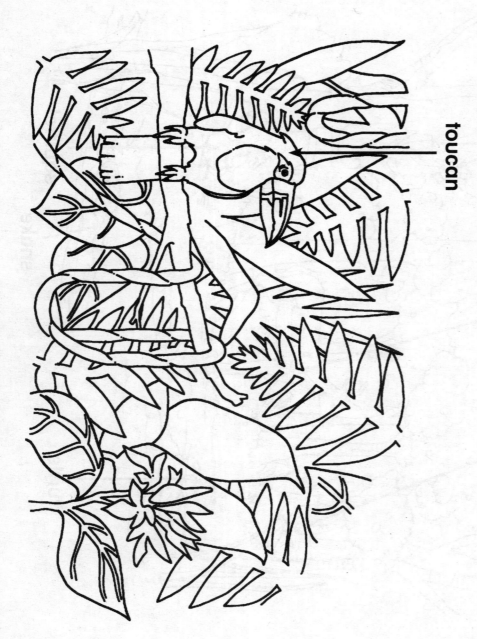

toucan

www.harcourtschoolsupply.com

What Lives in Forests?

1. Draw a circle around 2 nonliving things.

2. Draw a box around 3 living things.

3. Color the part that shows where an animal might find water.

4. Draw an X on a place that an animal might use for shelter.

www.harcourtschoolsupply.com
© Houghton Mifflin Harcourt Publishing Company

Life Science
Core Skills Science, G1 SV 9781419098413

What Lives in Forests?

Write your answers below.

5. Vocabulary What do you call a place

that has many trees close together?

_____

_____

6. Reading Skill Are all forests the same?

Tell how they are different.

_____

_____

7. Communicate Tell a partner how animals

use nonliving things.

_____

_____

What Lives in Oceans and Wetlands?

An ocean is a large body of salty water.

Animals and plants live in the ocean.

Ocean animals have special parts to help them live in water.

Fish have fins and tails to swim.

They have gills to breathe.

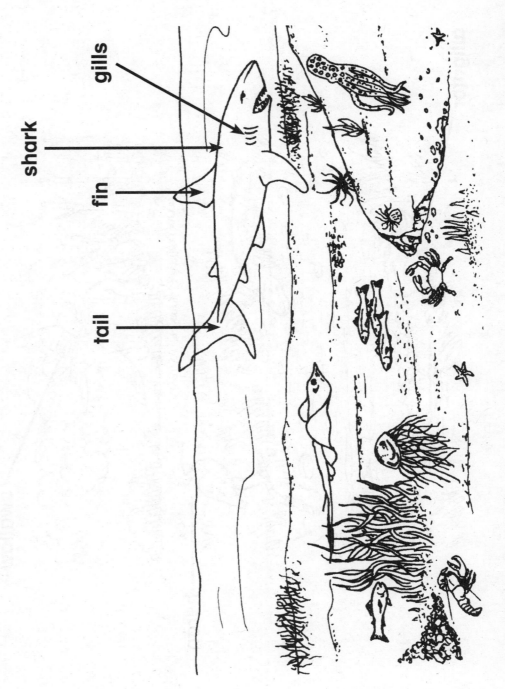

gills

shark

fin

tail

Life Science

Core Skills Science, G1 SV 9781419098413

www.harcourtschoolsupply.com

© Houghton Mifflin Harcourt Publishing Company

A wetland is land that is very wet.

There is mud in a wetland.

Many kinds of plants and animals live in a wetland.

The animals find food and water in the mud, water, and plants.

They find shelter in the mud, water, and plants.

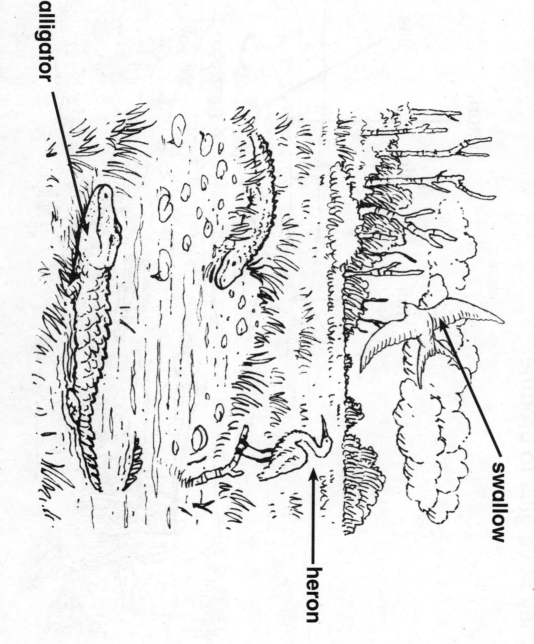

alligator

heron

swallow

Name _____

Date _____

What Lives in Oceans and Wetlands?

1. Draw a box around the ocean animals.

2. Draw a circle around the wetland animals.

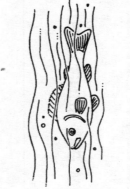

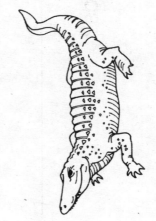

www.harcourtschoolsupply.com
© Houghton Mifflin Harcourt Publishing Company

Life Science
Core Skills Science, G1 SV 9781419098413

Name _____ Date _____

What Lives in Oceans and Wetlands?

Write your answers below.

3. Vocabulary What is a large body of

salty water called?

_____

_____

4. Reading Skill How are oceans different

from wetlands?

_____

_____

_____

5. Compare How are oceans like wetlands?

_____

_____

www.harcourtschoolsupply.com
© Houghton Mifflin Harcourt Publishing Company

Core Skills Science, G1 SV 9781419098413

Life Science

What Lives in a Desert?

A desert is a hot place with very little water.

It can be hard to find food and water.

It is hot during the day.

It is cool at night.

Many animals sleep during the day.

They look for food at night.

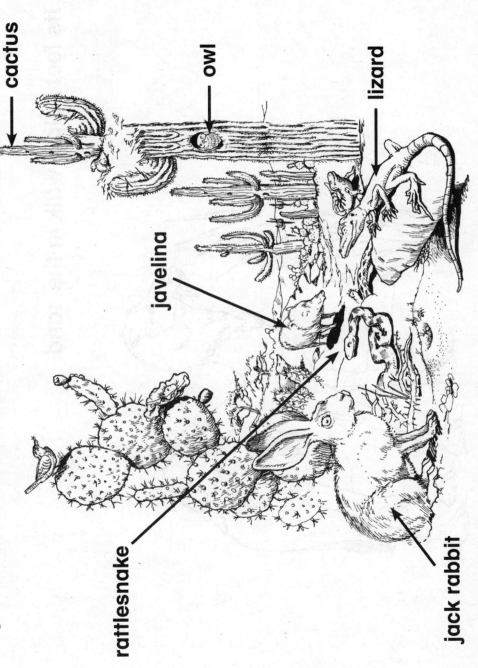

cactus

owl

lizard

javelina

rattlesnake

jack rabbit

Life Science

Core Skills Science, G1 SV 9781419098413

www.harcourtschoolsupply.com
© Houghton Mifflin Harcourt Publishing Company

Desert plants and animals have special parts.

The parts help them live in dry places.

A cactus has thick stems.

It has waxy skin.

The stems and skin hold water.

A camel has wide feet.

Its feet help it walk in the sand.

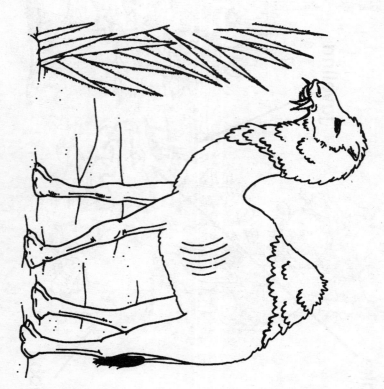

www.harcourtschoolsupply.com
© Houghton Mifflin Harcourt Publishing Company

What Lives in a Desert?

Label each picture with a word from the box.

| cactus | owl | rattlesnake | jack rabbit |

1.

2.

3.

4.

Underline the word that makes the sentence true.

5. A (desert, cactus) is a place with very little water.

6. The air in a desert can be hot or (wet, cold).

7. Many desert animals look for food at (night, noon) when the air is cool.

What Lives in a Desert?

Write your answers below.

8. Vocabulary What is a place with

very little water called?

_____

_____

9. Reading Skill Why do many desert

plants have waxy skins?

_____

_____

10. Infer Where do most desert animals stay

during the day?

_____

_____

What Covers Earth?

A natural resource is something from Earth that people use.

Water is a natural resource.

People use water in many ways.

People drink water.

People swim in water.

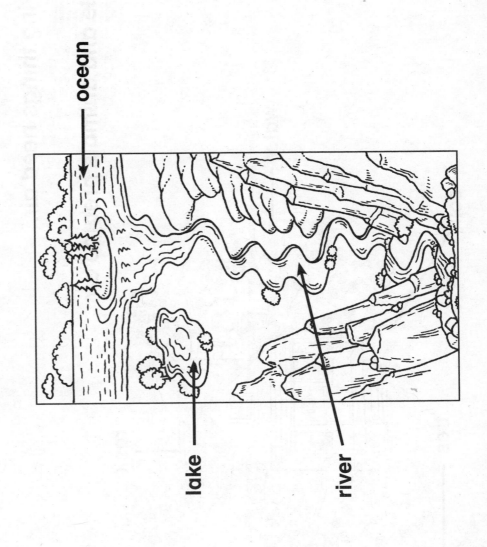

ocean

lake

river

Land is a natural resource.

Land includes soil, rocks, and sand.

People use soil to grow plants.

They use rocks to make buildings.

They use sand to make glass.

Air is a natural resource.

All living things need air.

People and animals breathe air.

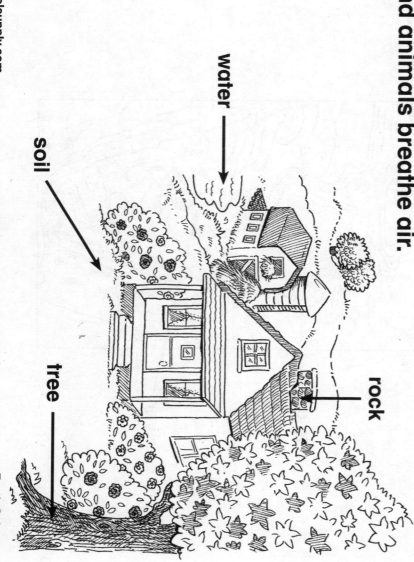

water

soil

tree

rock

Core Skills Science, G1 SV 9781419098413

Earth Science

Name _____   Date _____

What Covers Earth?

Draw a line from each word

to its picture.

1. Air

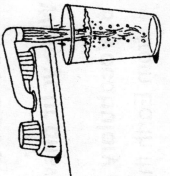

2. Land

3. Water

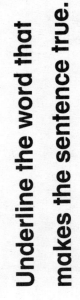

Underline the word that

makes the sentence true.

4. A natural resource is something

from Earth that people (play with, use).

5. Soil and rocks are (land, water) resources.

www.harcourtschoolsupply.com
© Houghton Mifflin Harcourt Publishing Company

Earth Science
Core Skills Science, G1 SV 9781419098413

What Covers Earth?

Write your answers below.

6. Vocabulary What do you call something

from Earth that people use?

_____

_____

7. Reading Skill How are water and land

resources alike? How are they different?

_____

_____

_____

8. Infer Why is a rock a natural resource?

_____

_____

_____

What Is Soil?

Soil is the top layer of Earth.

Soil is made of bits of minerals and rocks.

It is made of rotting plants and animals.

Soil has air and water in it, too.

Most plants grow in soil.

Some animals live in soil.

They help break
it into pieces.

This makes room
for air and
water.

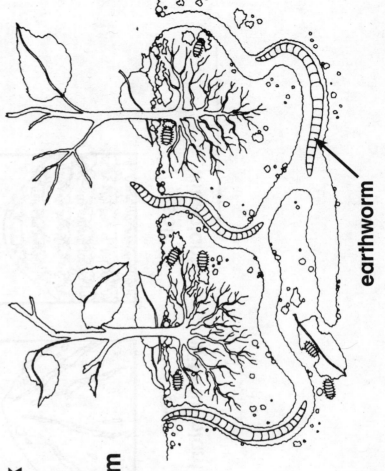

earthworm

Soil is a natural resource.

A natural resource is something from
Earth that people use.

We need to save soil.

Wind and water can take soil away.

Plants can save soil.

Plant roots hold soil in place.

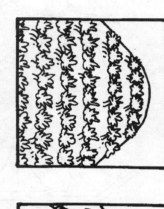

**soil
with plants**

**soil
without plants**

Name _____ Date _____

What Is Soil?

Match the sentences to the picture.

Write the numbers 1–3 on the picture.

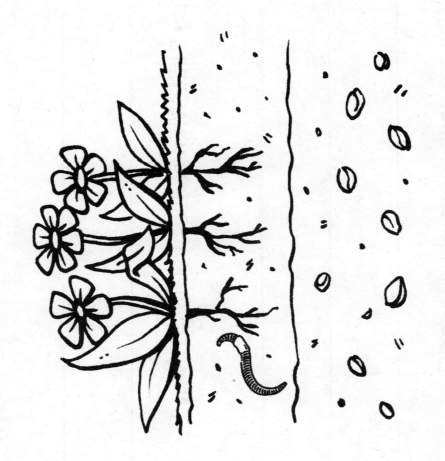

1. This helps hold soil in place.

2. This helps break soil into pieces.

3. This is Earth's loose top layer.

www.harcourtschoolsupply.com
© Houghton Mifflin Harcourt Publishing Company

Earth Science
Core Skills Science, G1 SV 9781419098413

Name _____   Date _____

What Is Soil?

Write your answers below.

4. Vocabulary What is soil?

_____

_____

5. Reading Skill What causes soil to go away?

_____

_____

_____

6. Infer Why are earthworms good for soil?

_____

_____

_____

www.harcourtschoolsupply.com
© Houghton Mifflin Harcourt Publishing Company

How Can We Help Earth?

A natural resource is something from Earth that people use.

Water, trees, and air are natural resources.

You can help save natural resources.

You can reuse, or use something again.

Reuse a milk jug.

You can make a bird feeder with it.

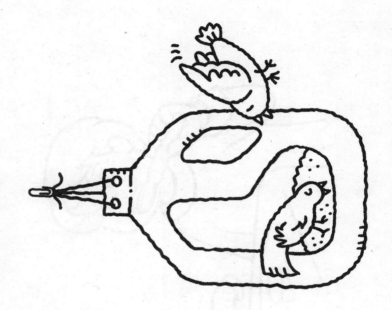

www.harcourtschoolsupply.com
© Houghton Mifflin Harcourt Publishing Company

Core Skills Science, G1 SV 9781419098413

Earth Science

You can recycle.

A new object is made from something old when you recycle.

You can recycle old cans.

Old cans are made into new cans.

You can reduce, or use less of something.

You can turn off water while you brush your teeth.

www.harcourtschoolsupply.com
© Houghton Mifflin Harcourt Publishing Company

How Can We Help Earth?

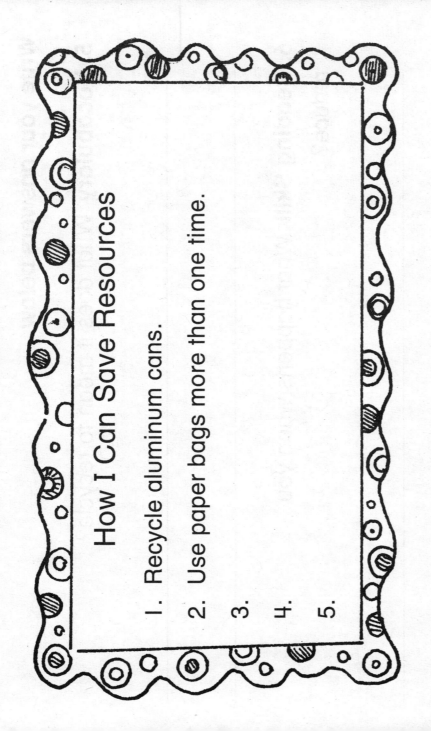

How I Can Save Resources

1. Recycle aluminum cans.

2. Use paper bags more than one time.

3.

4.

5.

Circle the number of the sentences that should go on the poster.

1. Use empty food cans to make pencil holders.

2. Keep the lights on.

3. Put newspapers in the recycling bin.

4. Buy larger packages instead of smaller ones.

How Can We Help Earth?

Write your answers below.

5. Vocabulary What does it mean to recycle?

_____

_____

6. Reading Skill What happens when you reduce?

_____

_____

7. Classify Do you reuse, recycle, or reduce when you use an old can as a trash can?

_____

_____

How Can You Measure Weather?

Weather is what the air outside is like.

You can use tools to tell about weather.

A thermometer measures temperature.

Temperature is how warm or cool something is.

You wear warm clothes when the temperature is cold.

You wear lighter clothes when the temperature is hot.

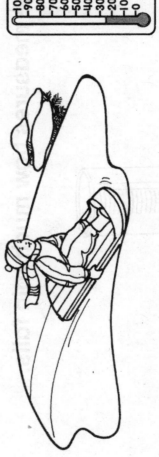

You can use a tool to measure wind.

A windsock shows which way the wind blows.

It shows how hard the wind blows, too.

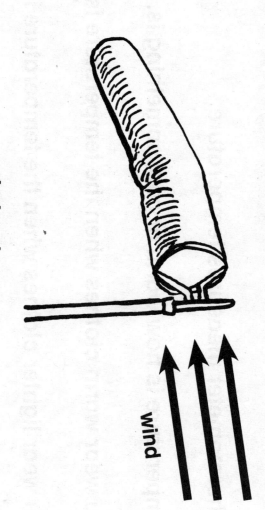

windsock

wind

You can use a tool to measure rain.

A rain gauge measures how much rain falls.

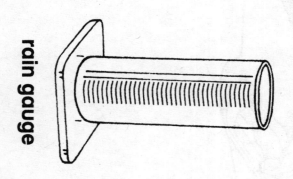

rain gauge

How Can You Measure Weather?

Draw a line from each definition
to the tool it tells about.

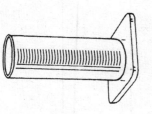

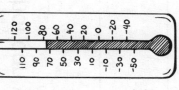

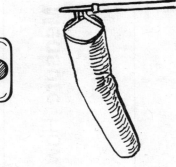

1. a tool that measures
temperature

2. a tool to measure
the wind

3. a tool to measure
how much rain falls

How Can You Measure Weather?

Write your answers below.

4. Vocabulary What is temperature?

_____

_____

5. Reading Skill If a windsock is hanging down, what can you tell about the wind?

_____

_____

6. Measure How can you describe weather?

_____

_____

What Are Clouds and Rain?

A water cycle is when water moves from Earth to the sky and back again.

The sun warms water.

Some warm water goes into the air.

You cannot see it.

Water in the air cools.

Tiny drops of water make up a cloud.

Some drops get bigger.

The drops fall to Earth as rain.

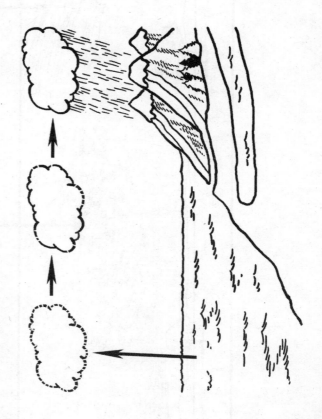

Core Skills Science, G1 SV 9781419098413

www.harcourtschoolsupply.com
© Houghton Mifflin Harcourt Publishing Company

Look at clouds to see how weather changes.

Some clouds are thin.

It may rain in a day or two.

Some clouds are puffy and white.

They can turn gray and bring rain.

Some clouds are low and gray.

They may bring rain or snow.

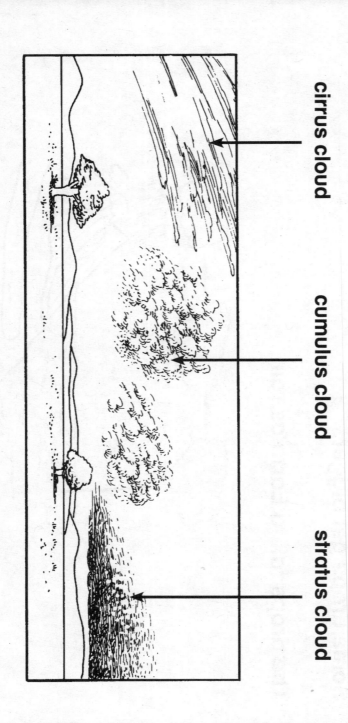

cirrus cloud

cumulus cloud

stratus cloud

www.harcourtschoolsupply.com
© Houghton Mifflin Harcourt Publishing Company

Name _____

Date _____

What Are Clouds and Rain?

Match the steps to the picture. Write the numbers 1–3 on the picture.

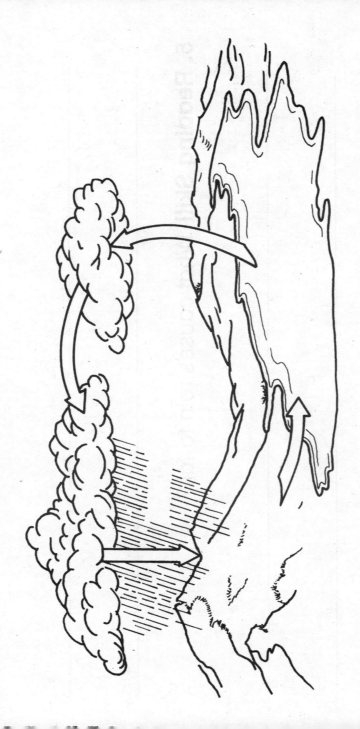

Steps of the Water Cycle

1. Heat from the Sun causes water to go into the air.

2. Tiny drops of water in the air form clouds.

3. Water falls back to Earth as rain or sleet.

What Are Clouds and Rain?

Write your answers below.

4. Vocabulary What is the water cycle?

_____

_____

5. Reading Skill What causes rain to fall?

_____

_____

6. Compare Draw two kinds of clouds.
Tell how they are alike and different.

_____

_____

_____

What Is Weather Like in Spring and Summer?

A season is a time of year.

It has its own kind of weather.

Spring is the season that follows winter.

It is warmer in spring.

Warm weather and rain help plants begin to grow.

Animals that were sleeping in winter wake up.

Many baby animals are born in spring.

Core Skills Science, G1 SV 9781419098413

www.harcourtschoolsupply.com
© Houghton Mifflin Harcourt Publishing Company

Summer is the season that follows spring.

Summer is the warmest season.

People wear clothing that keeps them cool.

Plants grow in summer.

Young animals grow bigger and learn to find food.

Soon fall comes.

The seasons change in the same order — spring, summer, fall, and winter.

www.harcourtschoolsupply.com
© Houghton Mifflin Harcourt Publishing Company

Name _____

Date _____

What Is Weather Like in Spring and Summer?

Draw lines to match each phrase to a season.

1. season that follows winter

2. people try to keep cool

3. rain helps new plants grow

4. the warmest season

5. young animals grow bigger

6. many baby animals are born

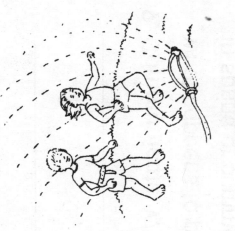

spring

summer

Earth Science
Core Skills Science, G1 SV 9781419098413

www.harcourtschoolsupply.com
© Houghton Mifflin Harcourt Publishing Company

Name _____ Date _____

What Is Weather Like in Spring and Summer?

Write your answers below.

7. Vocabulary What is a season?

_____

_____

8. Reading Skill How are spring and summer alike?

_____

_____

9. Communicate Write a story telling what happens to plants or animals in spring or summer.

_____

_____

What Is Weather Like in Fall and Winter?

A season is a time of year.

It has its own kind of weather.

Fall is the season that follows summer.

It is cooler in fall.

People wear warmer clothes.

Leaves drop from trees.

Animals get ready for colder weather.

Some animals grow thick fur.

Many animals store food for winter.

www.harcourtschoolsupply.com
© Houghton Mifflin Harcourt Publishing Company

Earth Science
Core Skills Science, G1 SV 9781419098413

Winter is the season that follows fall.

It is the coldest season.

Snow falls in some places.

Sometimes it is hard for animals to find food.

Some plants die.

Soon spring comes again.

The seasons change in the same order — spring, summer, fall, and winter.

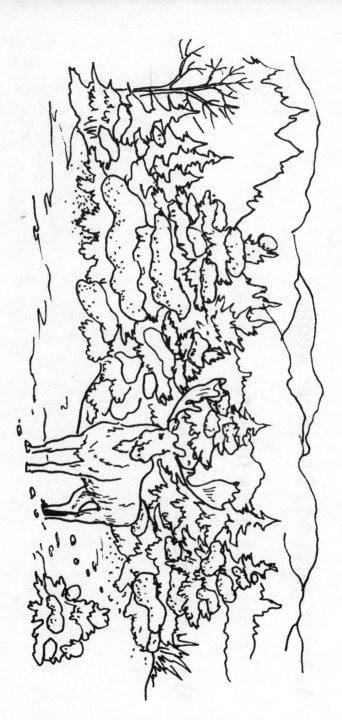

Name _____ Date _____

What Is Weather Like in Fall and Winter?

Draw lines to match each phrase to a season.

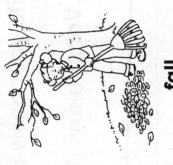

fall

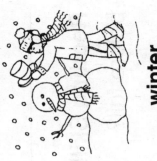

winter

1. weather gets cooler

2. some plants die

3. coldest season

4. animals grow thick fur

Use words from the box to name the seasons.

spring	summer	fall	winter

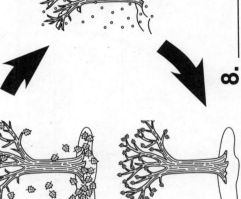

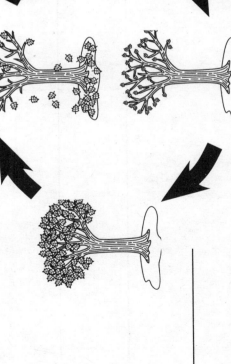

5. _____

6. _____

7. _____

8. _____

www.harcourtschoolsupply.com
© Houghton Mifflin Harcourt Publishing Company

Earth Science
Core Skills Science, G1 SV 9781419098413

What Is Weather Like in Fall and Winter?

Write your answers below.

9. Vocabulary What is winter?

_____

_____

10. Reading Skill What season comes before fall?

_____

_____

11. Classify Name three signs of fall.

_____

_____

_____

www.harcourtschoolsupply.com

Earth Science
Core Skills Science, G1 SV 9781419098413

What Can You See in the Sky?

The day sky is light.

You may see clouds and birds.

You may see the Sun, too.

The Sun is the brightest object in the day sky.

It warms the land and water.

It warms the air.

You will not see other stars in the day.

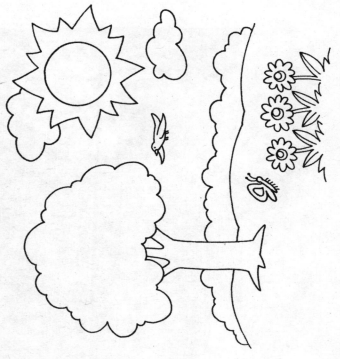

Earth Science

Core Skills Science, G1 SV 9781419098413

www.harcourtschoolsupply.com
© Houghton Mifflin Harcourt Publishing Company

The night sky is dark.

There is no light from the Sun.

You can see the Moon and stars at night.

Sometimes you can see planets.

A planet is an object that moves around the Sun.

Earth is a planet.

www.harcourtschoolsupply.com
© Houghton Mifflin Harcourt Publishing Company

78

Name _____ Date _____

What Can You See in the Sky?

Draw a line from each picture to its definition.

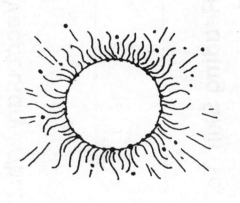

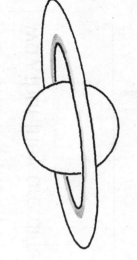

1. a space object that moves around the Sun

2. a space object that you can see in the night sky

3. the brightest space object in the sky

Underline the word that makes the sentence true.

4. The (day, night) sky is light.

5. The (day, night) sky is dark.

Earth Science

Core Skills Science, G1 SV 9781419098413

www.harcourtschoolsupply.com
© Houghton Mifflin Harcourt Publishing Company

Name _____ Date _____

What Can You See in the Sky?

Write your answers below.

6. Vocabulary What makes the day sky bright?

_____

_____

7. Reading Skill Tell one way that the Sun and the Moon are alike. Tell one way that they are different.

_____

_____

8. Observe Tell what you see in the sky.

_____

_____

What Causes Day and Night?

Earth rotates, or spins.

The Sun shines on different parts
of Earth as it spins.

It is day when the part of Earth
where you live faces the Sun.

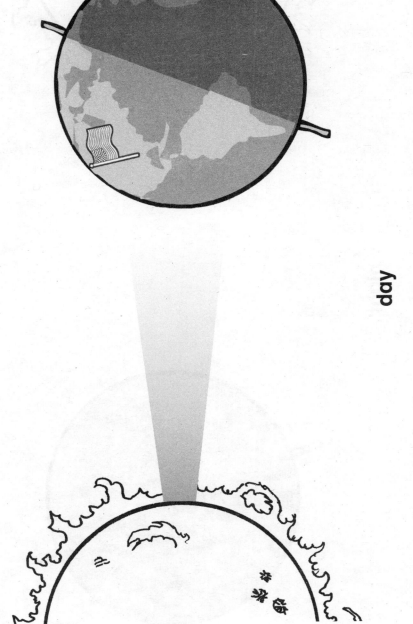

day

www.harcourtschoolsupply.com
© Houghton Mifflin Harcourt Publishing Company

81

Earth Science
Core Skills Science, G1 SV 9781419098413

It is night when the part of Earth where you live faces
away from the Sun.

It takes 24 hours for Earth to rotate one time.

Earth keeps rotating.

Day and night repeat.

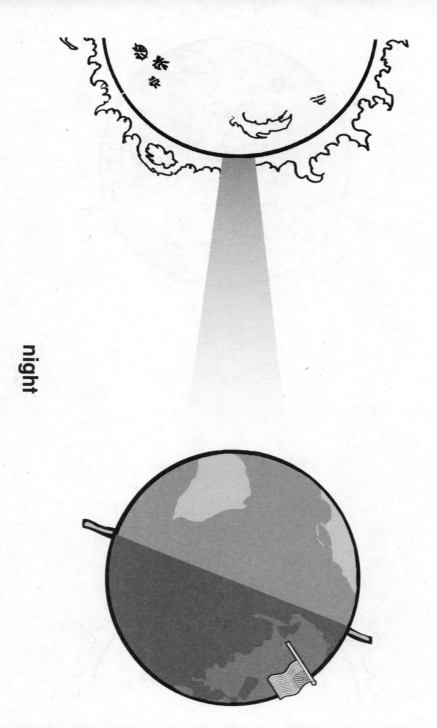

night

www.harcourtschoolsupply.com
© Houghton Mifflin Harcourt Publishing Company

Name _____ Date _____

What Causes Day and Night?

1. Label the picture using words from the box.

night	day	rotates

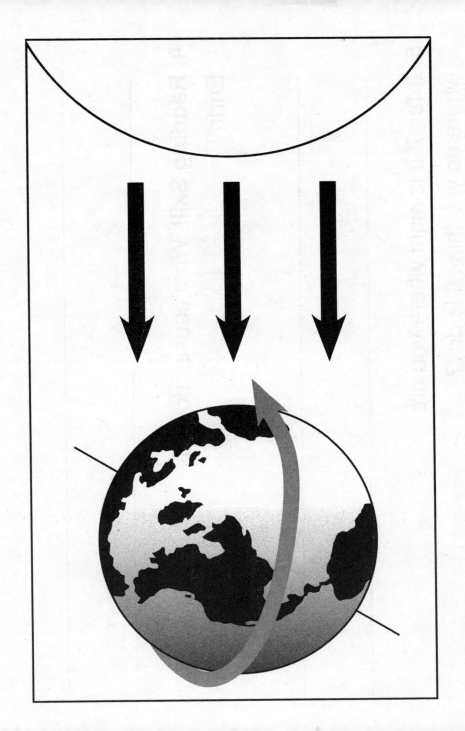

Underline the word that makes the sentence true.

2. It takes one (hour, day) for Earth to rotate one time.

Earth Science
Core Skills Science, G1 SV 9781419098413

What Causes Day and Night?

Write your answers below.

3. Vocabulary How does Earth move

when it rotates?

_____

_____

4. Reading Skill What causes day on

Earth?

_____

_____

5. Infer If it is night where you are,

where do you think it is day?

_____

_____

How Do the Moon and Sun Seem to Change?

The Moon is a round object that moves around Earth.

The Moon does not make light.

The Sun is a star that makes its own light.

The Sun shines on the Moon so we can see it.

The Moon seems to change its size and shape each night.

We see the part of the Moon that the Sun is shining on.

These different shapes are called the phases of the Moon.

Phases of the Moon

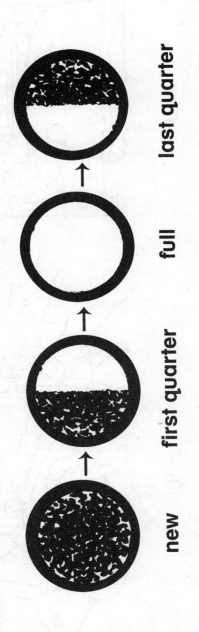

new   first quarter   full   last quarter

Earth Science

Core Skills Science, G1 SV 9781419098413

www.harcourtschoolsupply.com

© Houghton Mifflin Harcourt Publishing Company

The Sun seems to change, too.

It seems to move from one side of the sky to the other.

The Sun is not moving.

Earth is rotating and moving.

The Sun is low in the sky in the morning.

It is high in the sky at noon.

It is low in the sky late in the day.

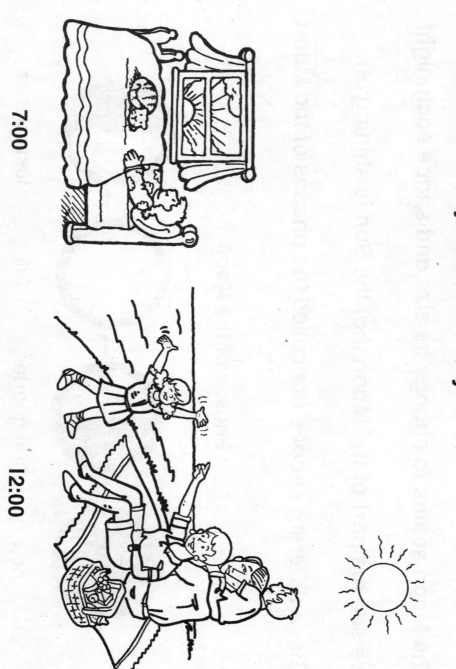

7:00

12:00

Core Skills Science, G1 SV 9781419098413

Earth Science

Name _____ Date _____

How Do the Moon and Sun Seem to Change?

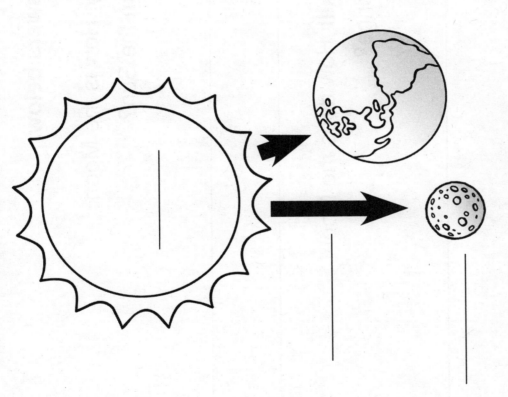

Match the sentences to the picture.

Write the numbers 1–3 on the lines.

1. The Sun is a star that shines on the Moon.

2. Light from the Sun lets us see the Moon.

3. We see the part of the Moon that the Sun
   is shining on.

How Do the Moon and Sun Seem to Change?

Write your answers below.

4. Vocabulary How is the Moon

different from the Sun?

_____

_____

5. Reading Skill How does the Moon

seem to change?

_____

_____

6. Reading Skill What happens to the

Sun in the sky as Earth rotates?

_____

_____

How Can You Describe Matter?

Matter is what all things are made of.

You use your senses to learn about matter.

You can see popcorn.

You can smell it.

You can touch it.

You can hear it crunch.

You can even taste it!

Physical Science

Core Skills Science, G1 SV 9781419098413

You can use your senses to tell about a property of a thing.

A property is anything you learn about an object by using your senses.

You can see the color, size, and shape of things.

You can hear how things sound.

You can tell how some things taste.

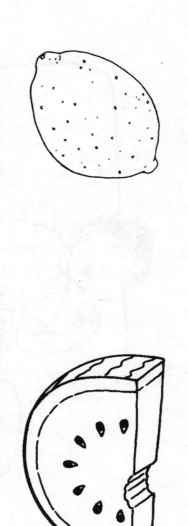

sour

sweet

Name _____

Date _____

How Can You Describe Matter?

Draw a line from each word to its picture.

1. large

2. small

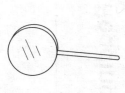

3. soft

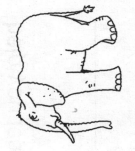

4. rough

5. salty

6. sweet

How Can You Describe Matter?

Write your answers below.

7. Vocabulary What is matter?

_____

_____

8. Reading Skill How can your senses

help you learn about matter?

_____

_____

9. Classify Look at the picture.
Name two of its properties.

_____

_____

What Are Solids, Liquids, and Gases?

Matter is what all things are made of.

There are three forms of matter.

Matter can be a solid, liquid, or gas.

A solid is matter that has its own shape.

A table and paper are kinds of solids.

You can change a solid's shape.

You can cut it.

You can break it.

solid

Physical Science
Core Skills Science, G1 SV 9781419098413

www.harcourtschoolsupply.com
© Houghton Mifflin Harcourt Publishing Company

A liquid is matter that flows.

It takes the shape of what it is in.

Water is a liquid.

liquid

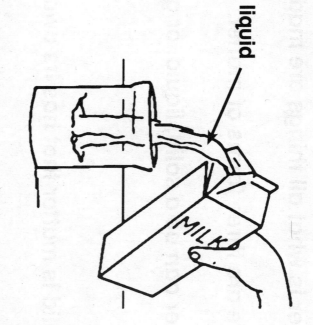

A gas is matter that changes shape to fill all the space of what it is in.

The air around you is a gas.

Gas is inside balloons, too.

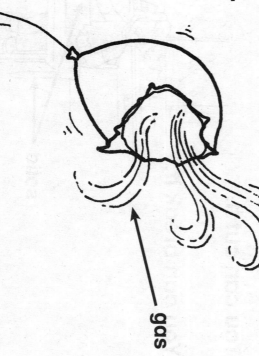

gas

Name _____ Date _____

What Are Solids, Liquids, and Gases?

Draw a line from each phrase to its picture.

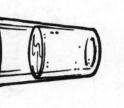

1. has its own shape

2. fills all the space it is in

3. flows and takes the shape of its container

Underline the word that makes the sentence true.

4. Matter is what (some, all) things are made of.

5. The air around you is a (solid, gas).

Physical Science
Core Skills Science, G1 SV 9781419098413
www.harcourtschoolsupply.com
© Houghton Mifflin Harcourt Publishing Company

What Are Solids, Liquids, and Gases?

Write your answers below.

6. Vocabulary What is a solid?

_____

_____

7. Reading Skill What form of matter are milk, juice, and water?

_____

_____

8. Compare How are solids, liquids, and gases different?

_____

_____

What Do Heating and Cooling Do?

Water can change from one form of matter to another.

Water freezes when it is very cold.

To freeze is to change from a liquid to a solid.

Ice is solid water.

Solids can melt when they are heated.

To melt is to change from a solid to a liquid.

Ice melts when it gets warm.

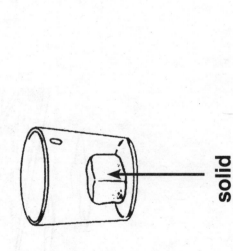

liquid

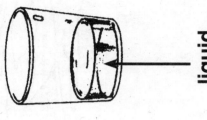

solid

Physical Science

Core Skills Science, G1 SV 9781419098413

www.harcourtschoolsupply.com

© Houghton Mifflin Harcourt Publishing Company

Water can be a gas, too.

Water evaporates when it is heated.

To evaporate is to change from a liquid to a gas.

You do not see water when it is a gas.

Heat from the Sun makes water evaporate.

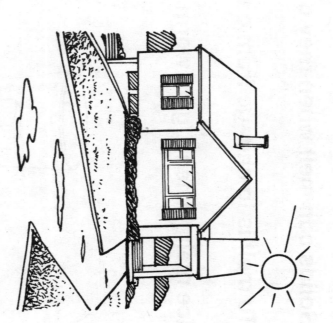

What Do Heating and Cooling Do?

1. Circle the word that tells what happened to the ice cube.

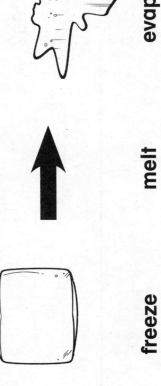

freeze   melt   evaporate

2. Circle the word that tells what happened to the water in the tray.

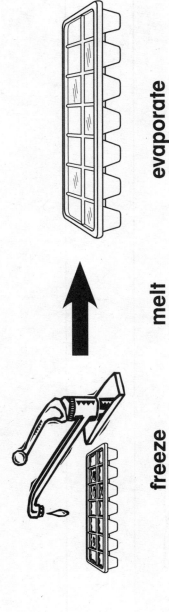

freeze   melt   evaporate

3. Circle the word that tells what happened to the water puddle.

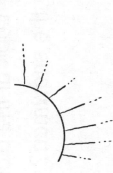

freeze   melt   evaporate

www.harcourtschoolsupply.com
© Houghton Mifflin Harcourt Publishing Company

Physical Science
Core Skills Science, G1 SV 9781419098413

Name _____   Date _____

What Do Heating and Cooling Do?

Write your answers below.

4. Vocabulary What happens when
water evaporates?

_____

_____

5. Reading Skill What causes liquid
water to change into ice?

_____

_____

6. Compare Look at the picture. What will
happen to the snowman? Why?

_____

_____

Physical Science
Core Skills Science, G1 SV 9781419098413

Where Does Heat Come From?

Energy is something that can cause change or do work.

Heat is a kind of energy.

Heat makes things warm.

The Sun gives off heat.

The Sun warms the air, water, and land.

A light bulb gives off heat.

A fire gives off heat, too.

101

Physical Science
Core Skills Science, G1 SV 9781419098413

Heat can make things change.

Heat makes ice melt.

Heat cooks food.

Heat from a fire warms you.

www.harcourtschoolsupply.com
© Houghton Mifflin Harcourt Publishing Company

Name _____

Where Does Heat Come From?

Look at each pair of pictures. Circle the thing that has been changed by heat.

1.

2.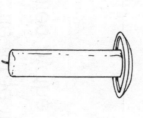

3.

4.

Physical Science

Core Skills Science, G1 SV 9781419098413

www.harcourtschoolsupply.com
© Houghton Mifflin Harcourt Publishing Company

Where Does Heat Come From?

Write your answers below.

5. Vocabulary What is energy?

_____

_____

6. Reading Skill Name three things on
Earth that are heated by the Sun.

_____

_____

7. Compare How is heat from the Sun
the same as heat from a fire?

_____

_____

Where Does Light Come From?

Light is a kind of energy.

Earth gets light from the Sun.

Fires and light bulbs give off light, too.

Light can pass through some things.

Light can pass through clear glass.

It can pass through air and water.

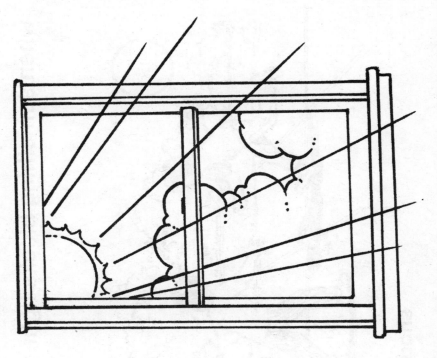

www.harcourtschoolsupply.com
© Houghton Mifflin Harcourt Publishing Company

Physical Science
Core Skills Science, G1 SV 9781419098413

Some things let a little light through.

Sunglasses let a little light through.

Light does not pass through all things.

Some things stop all light.

Curtains can stop light.

Your body stops light, too.

A dark shape called a shadow forms
when something blocks light.

shadow

Name _____

Date _____

Where Does Light Come From?

1. Circle the things that give off light. Draw a box around the thing that does not give off light.

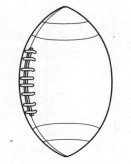  

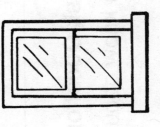 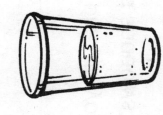 

2. Write a P on the things that light can pass through. Write an S on the thing that makes a shadow.

Physical Science
Core Skills Science, G1 SV 9781419098413

www.harcourtschoolsupply.com
© Houghton Mifflin Harcourt Publishing Company

Name _____ Date _____

Where Does Light Come From?

Write your answers below.

3. **Vocabulary** What kind of energy can

you see?

_____

_____

4. **Reading Skill** Why can you see

a shadow?

_____

_____

5. **Ask Questions** What else do you want

to know about light and shadows?

_____

_____

How Is Sound Made?

Sound is a kind of energy that you can hear.

Sound is made when something vibrates.

To vibrate means to move back and forth very fast.

You make a sound when you talk.

Place your hand on your neck.

Now sing or talk.

You can feel your neck vibrate.

Physical Science

Core Skills Science, G1 SV 9781419098413

www.harcourtschoolsupply.com

© Houghton Mifflin Harcourt Publishing Company

How can you hear sound?

Think about a drum.

A drum vibrates when you hit it.

The air around the drum vibrates, too.

Air that vibrates makes parts inside your ear vibrate.

Then you hear sound.

www.harcourtschoolsupply.com
© Houghton Mifflin Harcourt Publishing Company

Name _____

Date _____

How Is Sound Made?

1. Write an S on the objects that are making sound.

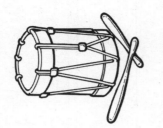 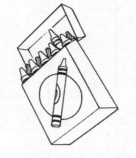

Circle the word that makes the sentence true.

2. The kind of energy you can hear is called (sound, light).

3. Sound is made when something (vibrates, shines).

Physical Science
Core Skills Science, G1 SV 9781419098413

www.harcourtschoolsupply.com
© Houghton Mifflin Harcourt Publishing Company

Name _____ Date _____

How Is Sound Made?

Write your answers below.

4. Vocabulary What is sound?

_____

_____

5. Reading Skill How do you hear sound?

_____

_____

_____

6. Observe If you see something vibrate, what will you hear?

_____

_____

www.harcourtschoolsupply.com
© Houghton Mifflin Harcourt Publishing Company

How Are Sounds Different?

Not all sounds are the same.

Pitch is how high or low a sound is.

Fast vibrations make a high pitch.

Most small things make sounds that have a high pitch.

Slow vibrations make a low pitch.

Most big things make sounds that have a low pitch.

low pitch

high pitch

www.harcourtschoolsupply.com
© Houghton Mifflin Harcourt Publishing Company

A sound can be different because of its volume.

Volume is how loud or soft a sound is.

It takes little energy to make a soft sound.

A whisper is a soft sound.

It takes lots of energy to make a loud sound.

A blowing whistle is a loud sound.

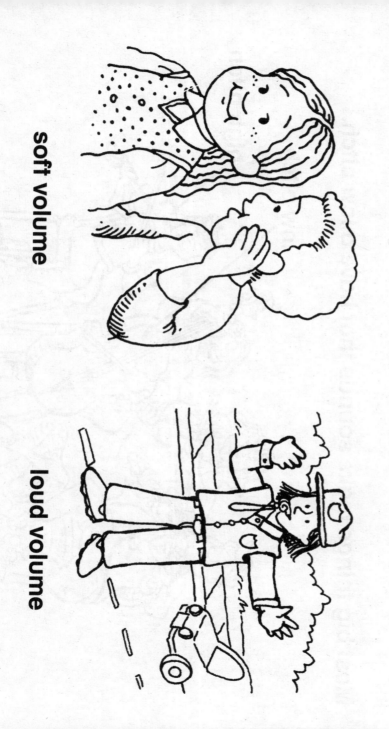

soft volume

loud volume

www.harcourtschoolsupply.com
© Houghton Mifflin Harcourt Publishing Company

Name _____

Date _____

How Are Sounds Different?

Draw lines to match each phrase to its picture.

1. high pitch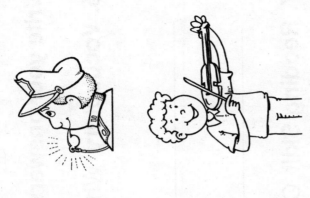

2. low pitch

3. high volume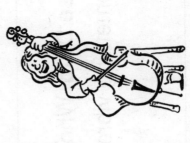

4. low volume

Circle the word that makes the sentence true.

5. The faster something vibrates, the (lower, higher) the sound.

www.harcourtschoolsupply.com
© Houghton Mifflin Harcourt Publishing Company

Physical Science
Core Skills Science, G1 SV 9781419098413

How Are Sounds Different?

Write your answers below.

6. Vocabulary What is volume?

_____

_____

7. Reading Skill Compare loud and soft sounds.

_____

_____

8. Use Data What does how fast or slow something vibrates tell about pitch?

_____

_____

What Makes Things Move?

A push is a force.

A force can move a thing.

A push is a force that moves something away.

People push you on a swing.

A pull is a force, too.

A pull is a force that moves something closer.

You pull a wagon

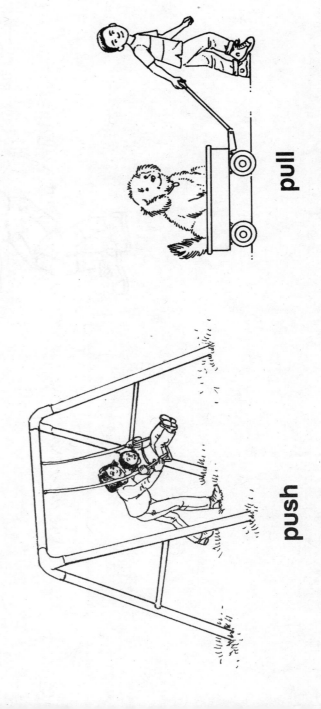

pull

push

Core Skills Science, G1 SV 9781419098413

www.harcourtschoolsupply.com
© Houghton Mifflin Harcourt Publishing Company

Gravity is a force that pulls things toward Earth's center.

You fall down when you trip.

Gravity pulls you to the ground.

A ball falls when you throw it.

Gravity pulls it to the ground.

Name _____

Date _____

What Makes Things Move?

Draw a line from each word to its picture.

1. pull

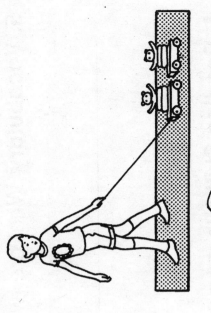

2. gravity

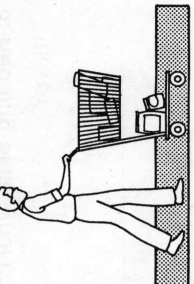

3. push

4. Draw a circle around the pictures above that show a force.

Physical Science
Core Skills Science, G1 SV 9781419098413
www.harcourtschoolsupply.com
© Houghton Mifflin Harcourt Publishing Company

What Makes Things Move?

Write your answers below.

5. Vocabulary What are two kinds of force?

_____

_____

6. Reading Skill What causes objects to move?

_____

_____

7. Communicate How would you explain gravity to a friend?

_____

_____

_____

Why Are Things Fast and Slow?

Speed is how fast or slow something moves.

A train moves fast.

A snail moves slow.

Something that is moving from one place to another is in motion.

A force can change the motion of something.

You can make a ball roll faster if you kick it harder.

You stop a ball when you catch it.

www.harcourtschoolsupply.com
© Houghton Mifflin Harcourt Publishing Company

Physical Science
Core Skills Science, G1 SV 9781419098413

A ball is light.

It is easy to stop.

It is easy to move.

Some things are heavy.

Heavy things are hard to stop.

You have to use more force to stop them.

Heavy things are hard to move, too.

You have to use more force to move them.

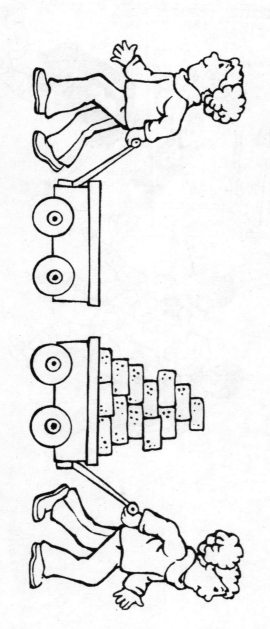

light

heavy

www.harcourtschoolsupply.com
© Houghton Mifflin Harcourt Publishing Company

Physical Science

Core Skills Science, G1 SV 9781419098413

Name _____   Date _____

Why Are Things Fast and Slow?

1. Circle the thing that moves at a slow speed.

2. Circle the picture that shows something changing direction.

3. Circle the thing that you will need more force to move.

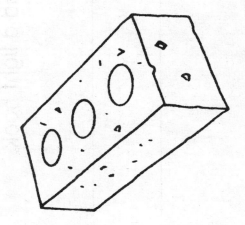 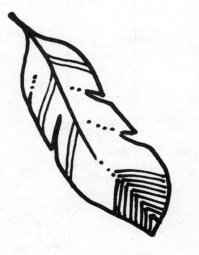

www.harcourtschoolsupply.com
© Houghton Mifflin Harcourt Publishing Company

Physical Science
Core Skills Science, G1 SV 9781419098413

Name _____   Date _____

Why Are Things Fast and Slow?

Write your answers below.

4. Vocabulary What word tells how fast or slow
an object moves?

_____

5. Reading Skill What are you doing when you
catch a ball?

_____

_____

6. Compare Compare moving a heavy book
and a light book.

_____

_____

Answer Key

Life Science

What are the Parts of Plants?

1. root
2. stem
3. leaf
4. flower
5. Stems
6. Leaves
7. The part of a plant that takes in water and holds the plant in the ground
8. to take in water that is in the ground and hold onto the ground
9. stems, leaves, flowers, and seeds

How Can Plants Be Sorted?

1. cactus
2. ivy
3. parts
4. people
5. seeds
6. cactus
7. Animals eat seeds, fruit, and leaves.
8. Sample answer: Some plants have spines. Some plants have flat leaves.

How Do Plants Change As They Grow?

1. pinecone
2. seedling
3. seeds
4. the part in a pine tree that grows seeds
5. seedling
6. A model can show what a plant looks like at different times in its life cycle.

How Do Animals Use Their Parts?

1. owl
2. shark
3. owl and lion
4. fish
5. lion
6. Fins help a fish move in water.
7. Ears, eyes, legs, and paws help an animal find food.
8. A stinger hurts. It will make another animal go away.

How Are Animals Grouped?

1. frog: amphibian
   lizard: reptile
   wolf: mammal
   goldfish: fish
   bird: bird

2. bird
3. goldfish
4. Gills are the body part of a fish that help it breathe.
5. Birds and mammals both have lungs that help them breathe.
6. a frog

What Can People Do?

1. hand
2. nose
3. ears
4. eyes
5. mouth
6. Answers may vary.
7. eat good food, exercise, and sleep
8. Answers may vary.

What Is a Living Thing?

1. boy holding baby
2. squirrel
3. dog drinking
4. cat and kitten
5. something that grows, changes, and makes others like itself
6. Answers may vary.
7. Water is a nonliving thing. It moves and takes up space, but it does not need air or food. It cannot make more water.

What Do Living Things Need?

1. sun and flowers
2. giraffe
3. mouse
4. dog
5. plants, other animals, and some eat both
6. food (sunlight), water, air, and space
7. water

What Lives in Forests?

1. rocks and water
2. Possible answers: plants, trees, shrubs
3. pond
4. Possible answers: tree, bush
5. a forest
6. No; different forests have different plants and animals.
7. Sample answer: They use nonliving things for shelter.

What Lives in Oceans and Wetlands?

1. shark, crab, fish

2. hawk, alligator, heron (Please note that some students may mark crab or fish in wetlands as well.)
3. an ocean
4. An ocean is a large body of water. Wetlands have water and mud.
5. Both are wet places where plants and animals live.

What Lives in a Desert?

1. rattlesnake
2. cactus
3. jack rabbit
4. owl
5. desert
6. cold
7. night
8. a desert
9. to help them hold water
10. in their homes

Earth Science

What Covers Earth?

1. singer
2. gardener
3. water glass
4. use
5. land
6. a natural resource
7. Both are used by people. Water is used for drinking. Land is used to grow plants.
8. People can use it to build houses.

What Is Soil?

1. roots
2. earthworm
3. soil
4. the top layer of Earth
5. Water and wind cause the soil to go away.
6. Earthworms break up soil to make room for air and water.

How Can We Help Earth?

Circle 1, 3, and 4.
5. to make an object into something new
6. You use less of something.
7. reuse

Answer Key

www.harcourtschoolsupply.com
© Houghton Mifflin Harcourt Publishing Company
Core Skills Science, G1 SV 9781419098413

Answer Key

www.harcourtschoolsupply.com
© Houghton Mifflin Harcourt Publishing Company

How Can You Measure Weather?

1. thermometer
2. windsock
3. rain gauge
4. how cool or warm something is
5. No wind is blowing.
6. You can use tools to measure temperature, wind, or rain.

What Are Clouds and Rain?

1-3. Check labels.
4. when water moves from Earth to the sky and back to Earth
5. Drops of water in clouds get bigger.
6. Answers may vary.

What Is Weather Like in Spring and Summer?

Spring: 1, 3, 6
Summer: 2, 4, 5
7. a time of year with its own kind of weather
8. The air gets warm.
9. Answers may vary.

What Is Weather Like in Fall and Winter?

Fall: 1, 4
Winter: 2, 3
5. summer
6. fall
7. winter
8. spring
9. the coldest season of the year
10. summer
11. Weather is cooler, leaves fall from trees, and animals grow thick fur.

What Can You See in the Sky?

1. Saturn
2. Moon
3. Sun
4. day
5. night
6. the Sun
7. Both are found in the sky. The Sun gives off light, but the Moon doesn't.
8. Answers may vary.

What Causes Day and Night?

1. Check labels.
2. day
3. It spins.
4. the Sun shining on part of the Earth
5. It is day on the other side of the Earth.

How Do the Moon and Sun Seem to Change?

1. Sun
2. Light ray
3. Moon
4. The Sun makes its own light. The Moon does not.
5. It seems to change size and shape because of the way the Sun shines on it.
6. It seems to move across the sky.

Physical Science

How Can You Describe Matter?

1. elephant
2. mouse
3. rabbit
4. porcupine
5. popcorn
6. lollipop
7. what all things are made of
8. Your senses can help you find out how things taste, sound, feel, smell, and look.
9. Sample answers: light, soft, small

What Are Solids, Liquids, and Gases?

1. chair
2. balloon
3. glass
4. all
5. gas
6. matter that has its own shape
7. liquid
8. A solid has its own shape. Liquid and gases do not.

What Do Heating and Cooling Do?

1. melt
2. freeze
3. evaporate
4. It changes from a liquid to a gas.
5. Freezing turns water to ice.
6. The Sun heats the snowman. The snowman will melt.

Where Does Heat Come From?

1. melted ice cube
2. burning candle
3. burning logs
4. summer scene
5. something that can cause change or do work
6. air, land, and water
7. They both can warm up things.

Where Does Light Come From?

1. circle: candle, Sun
   box: football
2. P: glass, window; S: boy
3. light
4. Something blocks the light so it can't pass through.
5. Check questions.

How Is Sound Made?

1. singer, bell ringing, bird
2. sound
3. vibrates
4. a kind of energy that you can hear
5. Air that is vibrating enters the ear and makes parts in the ear vibrate.
6. You will hear a sound.

How Are Sounds Different?

1. violin
2. cello
3. whistle
4. whisper
5. higher
6. how loud or soft a sound is
7. Loud sounds take more energy to make than soft sounds.
8. If the vibration is fast, the pitch will be higher. If the vibration is slow, the pitch is lower.

What Makes Things Move?

1. wagon
2. tripping
3. shopping cart
4. wagon, shopping cart, tripping
5. a push and a pull
6. a force
7. Gravity is a force that pulls things down to the ground.

Why Are Things Fast and Slow?

1. snail
2. ball being kicked
3. brick
4. speed
5. You are stopping the ball and changing its motion.
6. A light book is easier to move than a heavy book.